E-SPORTS GAME DESIGN

by Cecilia Pinto McCarthy

NORWOOD HOUSE PRESS

Norwood House Press
P.O. Box 316598
Chicago, Illinois 60631

For information regarding Norwood House Press, please visit our website at:
www.norwoodhousepress.com or call 866-565-2900.

Content Consultant: Nick Tsirlis

LIBRARY OF CONGRESS CATALOGING-IN-PUBLICATION DATA

Names: McCarthy, Cecilia Pinto, author.
Title: E-sports game design / by Cecilia Pinto McCarthy.
Description: Chicago, Illinois : Norwood House Press, [2017] | Series:
    E-sports: game on! | Includes bibliographical references and index.

Identifiers: LCCN 2017009137 (print) | LCCN 2017021967 (ebook) | ISBN
    9781684041336 (eBook) | ISBN 9781599538921 (library edition : alk. paper)
Subjects: LCSH: Video games--Design--Juvenile literature. | Shared virtual
    environments--Juvenile literature.
Classification: LCC GV1469.3 (ebook) | LCC GV1469.3 .M383 2017 (print) | DDC
    794.8--dc23
LC record available at https://lccn.loc.gov/2017009137

302N—072017
Manufactured in the United States of America in North Mankato, Minnesota.

CONTENTS

Note: Words that are **bolded** in the text are defined in the glossary.

CHAPTER 1

The Evolution of Game Design

Can you imagine playing a video game at work? Some people get paid to. Video game production companies develop new video games. They hire quality assurance testers to examine video games before they are sold. It's the job of a quality assurance tester to play the games. They spend hours analyzing each part of a game. During a workday, testers check to make sure previous **bugs** or mistakes have been corrected. They test characters, levels, and other features. Do characters interact as they should? Are there issues with the levels? Most importantly, is the game fun to play? When an element doesn't work properly, the game tester communicates with people on the development team. Game designers, programmers, and artists fix the problems. Testing E-Sports

Trial and error and applying feedback are vital parts of the game testing process.

games is especially challenging. These games must be challenging for players and interesting for audiences to watch.

From Arcades to Arenas

The first commercially successful video game was called *Pong*. It was developed in 1972 by Atari, a company

Early consoles like this Atari 2600 brought gaming into the home.

created by engineers Nolan Bushnell and Ted Dabney. The simple black-and-white table tennis game was played on **arcade** machines. Its images were made from simple straight lines. *Pong*'s success helped launch the video game industry.

During the 1970s, the popularity of arcade and home game **consoles** took off. New video game production companies opened. They offered more complex games with more character actions. Game designers created games with increasing levels of difficulty to challenge player skills.

Advancements in computer technology in the 1980s and '90s increased the growth and popularity of video games. Game development companies like Nintendo and Sega emerged. These companies had teams that created video games for gaming consoles.

Nintendo created the game *Super Mario Bros.*, which presented players with multiple levels and character abilities. Games like

Games like *Super Mario Bros.* revolutionized game design.

Tennis for Two

Physicist William Higinbotham developed what many people consider the first video game in October 1958. Higinbotham was in charge of the electronics instruments lab at the Brookhaven National Laboratory in Upton, New York. Every year, the lab held a visitors' day, when the public could tour the lab. Higinbotham thought people might be bored just looking at machines. Using the lab's computer and other instruments, he created a simple game on a screen called *Tennis for Two.* Players turned a knob and pushed a button to bounce a dot "ball" over a line representing the net. The game was a success but never went beyond the lab.

these encouraged players to practice and improve their skills in order to advance to higher levels. Gaming became more widespread, and game development grew into a serious profit-making profession.

Initially, games could be created by one or two people. They did all the work, from coming up with an idea to programming and designing a game. More complex games meant more people were needed in the production process. Game development grew to include teams of people, such as programmers, designers, writers, artists, sound

Game design today almost always involves a team of collaborators.

DID YOU KNOW?

Engineer Ralph Baer invented and patented the first home video game console in 1971. Called Odyssey, it was a box that could be connected to a television set. Players inserted game cards and used controllers to operate dots and play games on the screen.

specialists, and many others.

Personal computers (PCs) and the Internet opened up a whole new era in gaming. Gamers could interact and compete against each other anywhere across the globe. Gaming became a social as well as virtual experience.

Players wanted games that let them be creative and expressive. They wanted games that were exciting and challenging. Most of all, they wanted games that let them interact with a broader community. Game developers responded with multilayered games. New games used rich **graphics** and competitive matchmaking systems. Players needed to have advanced skills to achieve higher rankings in the community.

Crash of '83

In 1983, the video game market crashed. One reason was the overproduction of game consoles. In 1982, Atari released its new 5200 console. But it didn't offer much more than the already available Atari 2600. Consequently, the Atari 5200 did not sell well. At the same time, companies were quickly producing millions of poorly designed games that no one wanted, games like Atari's *E.T. the Extra-Terrestrial.* Thousands of unsold game cartridges ended up being buried in a landfill in New Mexico.

Gamers can choose from many types of games, such as role-playing, shooter, strategy, and sports. Games used to be limited by the capabilities of technology. With today's advanced systems, designers

DID YOU KNOW?

Video games can be played on different platforms. A game platform is the system or hardware that is used to play the game. Some platforms include consoles such as Nintendo Wii U, Xbox One, and PlayStation 4. Smartphones and personal computers are also game platforms.

Modern game graphics show rich detail not possible in early games.

now primarily consider the game community and how to make a game that will be embraced.

DID YOU KNOW?

Japanese game designer Shigeru Miyamoto had much to do with the success of video game developer Nintendo. His games *Super Mario Bros.* and *The Legend of Zelda* are iconic within the video game industry. They appealed to players' sense of adventure, imagination, and curiosity.

CHAPTER 2

From Concept to Competition

Since the first video games were introduced, players have competed against one another. Even with the simplest games, players battled for the highest score. E-Sports represent the highest level of competitive video gaming. Game developers create E-Sports games with large-scale competition in mind. Their games must be not only fun for players but also entertaining for **spectators**. In fact, pleasing viewers is one of the most important aspects of E-Sports game design.

E-Sports players and spectators expect engaging and interactive environments. There must be challenging action. Games must sustain the audience's interest. It is essential for E-Sports games to be visually appealing and available to be broadcast to the gaming community. Successful games provide a satisfying game experience for both players and fans. Game design and development is a complex process. It involves a team of people performing a variety of tasks. It may take teams of up to 100 people several years to develop a single game.

The Concept

Step one in game design is the concept phase. All game development starts with an idea. E-Sports games are always developed with competition in mind. Ideas can originate anywhere and from anyone. A game designer or artist may come up with an idea on his or her own. Some companies hold brainstorming

Game ideas based off sports can make very popular E-Sports titles, like *FIFA 17* soccer seen here.

sessions. Stories may be based on real-life events. Sometimes game ideas come from other types of entertainment such as sports, movies, books, or board games.

However, many new ideas sprout from already-existing games. During the concept stage, designers consider the game's audience. A game with violence wouldn't be appropriate for young players. A **prototype** or game model

E-Sports games have fans that come watch, similar to other sports, and designers use fan input and experiences when designing games.

is completed to test the game concept. Developers want to make sure a game will be successful.

Designing for E-Sports

E-Sports game developers design games for both players and spectators. Successful games are exciting to play.

A well-designed game is easy to pick up and hard to put down. Winning players have physical and mental skill and stamina.

E-Sports fans want a game that is fun and thrilling to watch. Games cannot last too long or audience members may become bored. How long a game should last varies from game to game. Games must have an element of uncertainty. If the outcome is predictable, the game quickly loses appeal.

More than half of E-Sports players and spectators are between the ages of 18 and 34. This population means E-Sports games often have adult content such as violence. Games are played on large screens in arenas. Some fans watch games streamed on television or online. E-Sports games must have clear, easy-to-see visuals. Characters must be just the right size. They are drawn large enough to be seen clearly on a big screen without hiding other characters and objects. Scenes cannot be cluttered with too many units. Special effects like lightning strikes and explosions are precise and focused. This tells the audience

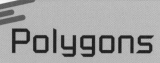

Polygons

The images in video games are made of flat shapes called polygons. Polygons have at least three lines. They can be triangles, rectangles, or other shapes. The polygons are used to make 3-D graphics. Rounded shapes are produced using several small polygons. To make a realistic image, color and texture are added onto the polygons.

when the target is hit. On-screen statistics help the audience track who is winning.

E-Sports games are different than traditional games. They are designed from the start to be used in E-Sports. This includes focus on multiplayer action and belonging to the gaming community.

Preproduction

Once an idea has been chosen, a preproduction team is formed. The team is made up of producers, designers, programmers, writers, and artists. They work together to flesh out details of the new game. The game designer oversees the project. He or she makes sure that all members of the development team work together to create the best game possible.

Writers craft a storyline. First, writers begin by writing a story summary. They describe the who, what, where, and how of the game. Characters, plot, settings, and themes come to life on paper. Writers also compose any dialogue or text that appears on screen.

A game design team storyboards a project just like a movie production team would.

Artists work with writers to create a storyboard. They draw rough sketches of characters and scenes. The storyboard explains what will happen in each part of the game. It combines the written text with artist sketches to describe what happens during the game.

Designers and programmers join in the storyboard process. They decide on the technical aspects of the game. They are concerned with how the game machine controls will affect what happens on screen. Many of the game details are worked out at this stage. A game design document or blueprint is finalized. These documents will guide the game production team throughout the development process.

CHAPTER 3

Putting a Game into Production

Production is the main stage of game development. At this point, more artists, designers, and programmers may be added to the development team. These additional team members are specialists in their fields. Feature designers work on components of the game, like mini games within the game. Assistant producers help keep the project on track.

Game Artists

Environmental artists create the video game's world. Using a computer, these artists make three-dimensional (3-D) models of the game's scenes. They may design cities, battlefields, or even alien worlds. Their work gives a feeling of depth and space to a game. Environmental artists make

A game artist considers intricate details when bringing a character to life.

sure that surfaces look wet or dry or that buildings shine in the sunlight.

Character artists draw incredibly detailed 3-D game characters. From humans to fantasy characters like dragons, character artists create beings that take on a life of their own. Characters may have wrinkles or dimples. They may be bald or hairy. The character artist makes sure every character is drawn accurately to reflect its personality. Artists also sometimes create costumes that the player can choose for the character. This allows players to become designers themselves and have fun interacting with the character.

Animators

Animators add motion and life to video games. They must make characters move realistically. This means deciding how characters react in different situations. If the story calls for a ninja character, players will expect the character to move sneakily.

Programmers

Programmers use computer languages to make video games work. They develop and use different types of **software** or codes. The codes are instructions that control how the game

DID YOU KNOW?

A game engine is a development tool that game designers can use to build a video game. It contains software that can be reused and adapted to create different games. Popular engines include Unity3D, Unreal, and CryEngine 3.

works. Many types of programmers are needed to create a video game. Each specializes in a particular area. Physics programmers control how characters and objects move in a game.

Artificial intelligence (AI) programmers figure out all the automated movements of characters and objects. They determine how characters interact with each other during a fight. They also come up with ways characters will move through different levels with human-controlled players.

Sound Designers

Sounds are an important part of the video game experience. Sound designers add every sound that goes into a video game. This includes voices, background noises,

Every function of a video game is contained within the game's code.

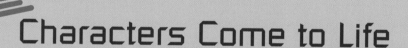

Characters Come to Life

Character riggers are specialists who make a game's characters come to life. They are responsible for the movements of characters and objects. Riggers must have knowledge of human anatomy. Using a computer program, the rigger makes a 3-D wire-frame skeleton of the character. Next, joints are added at points where the character will move. Riggers need to think about how movement of one body part affects other parts.

How a game is received by the gaming community ultimately decides the game's success or failure.

and even sounds on menu screens. Sound designers record real sounds or create sound effects.

Composers create music for the game. They make sure to create memorable music to immerse the player in the game. Composers work closely with the design team to make sure their music fits the gameplay.

Postproduction

At last, a game's art is finished, and all its code has been written. This first game edition is the alpha version. Now it's time for the play testers to try it out. Testers are members of the quality assurance team. They play video games over and over. They're looking for any mistakes or bugs. Testers report bugs to the production team. Programmers and artists review and correct any errors. Once the game's errors have been fixed, the improved game is called the beta version. The beta version goes through another round of play testing. Many beta versions today are released to the public for a short time. That way, the developer can really see how the game plays within the community. Finally, the game is released for sale.

Once a game is released, it belongs to the gaming community. It's up to them whether or not a game succeeds. Developers include features to help manage the community. Some games allow players to report others who use inappropriate language or violate other rules.

CHAPTER 4

Top Companies and Games

E-Sports competitions can involve multiplayer or one-on-one tournaments. There are four types or **genres** of E-Sports games. One of the most popular is the multiplayer online battle arena (MOBA) game. Players on two teams control one character each. Characters begin play with abilities that can improve over time. They advance toward each other on paths. To win, a team must destroy its opponent's main base.

Fighting Games involve characters in close combat with each other. In first-person shooter (FPS) games, the player sees the action through the eyes of the character. The character uses guns or other weapons to defeat an enemy. In real-time strategy games (RTS), players build armies and buildings on a map. Sometimes the goal is to take over as much map area as possible. Their goal is usually to destroy an opponent's base. While there are multiple companies designing E-Sports games, three of the top companies are Blizzard Entertainment, Valve, and Riot Games.

Blizzard Entertainment

Based in California, Blizzard Entertainment develops and publishes several popular E-Sports games. Its founders,

Members of a high school E-Sports team play *League of Legends*, a popular example of a MOBA game.

World of Warcraft by Blizzard Entertainment was the basis for the game *Hearthstone* and is a popular E-Sports game itself.

Michael Morhaime, Frank Pearce, and Allen Adham, started Blizzard in 1991. Two of Blizzard's best-known E-Sports titles are *Hearthstone* and *Overwatch*.

Hearthstone is a free-to-play game that is based on a previous Blizzard game called *World of Warcraft*. The game is designed around digital collectible cards. Players choose cards containing characters, abilities, and effects such as spells.

Creating *Hearthstone* was unusual and risky. It was a digital card game, which was not as popular as other games. At first, only two game designers, Eric Dodds and Ben Brode, worked on the project. They spent hours making paper playing cards and experimenting to get the game right. Dodds and Brode were joined by just 15 other staff members. They became known as Team 5. Team 5's small size was unusual. Most design teams at Blizzard had 60–100 people.

Team 5 was made up of people who loved collectible card games and had played them for decades. Various members worked on many game aspects, not just those in his or her special field. The team designed *Hearthstone* to be easy-to-learn with several **modes** of play. Players may play quick ten-minute games alone. They can also play against opponents online. Players collect cards to create powerful decks that enhance play possibilities.

Overwatch was a team-based multiplayer

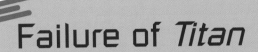

Failure of *Titan*

Not all game development projects end successfully. Blizzard Entertainment spent almost seven years and millions of dollars developing a game called *Titan*. But the project was canceled in September 2013. Many parts of the project were not working and coming together as they should. Game developers felt *Titan* was no longer worth finishing. It wasn't the first time Blizzard canceled a project. In fact, at least seven projects have been ended before they were completed. After the *Titan* failure, Blizzard put its energy into producing *Overwatch*.

first-person hero shooter game released in 2016. Unlike most games, *Overwatch* does not have a single player mode. It was designed to be played by two teams of six players each. The *Overwatch* characters are an international team of heroes. They join together to battle evil on futuristic Earth.

Overwatch creators have designed a game that is especially for E-Sports. It has all the factors necessary to become a successful E-sport. *Overwatch* is easy to learn and fun to play. It is based on teamwork and strategy. The characters have interesting backstories and individual personalities that players and fans love. These are attractive game qualities for both E-Sports players and fans. In fact, *Overwatch* had 20 million registered players worldwide in just its first five months.

Some members of the gaming community enjoy cosplay, or dressing up like their favorite characters, like these *Overwatch* fans.

Valve Corporation

Valve is an award-winning video game developer. It was founded by Gabe Newell and Mike Harrington. They formerly worked at the computer company Microsoft. Valve's first product was a successful FPS game called *Half-Life*, released in 1998. Their other popular titles include *Dota 2,* a MOBA game, and the multi-player FPS game *Counter-Strike: Global Offensive*.

Valve puts a great deal of emphasis on the importance of playtesting in game design. At Valve, like some other companies, game development involves repeated playtesting throughout the design process. Observers watch testers at play to understand how players interact with a game. They encourage testers to think out loud as they play. After testing, players are asked a number of questions about their experience. Testers also fill out surveys about the game.

Valve employee Mike Ambinder has a PhD in experimental psychology. His knowledge of psychology aids game design. By analyzing play testers' responses, Ambinder determines what creates a positive gaming experience.

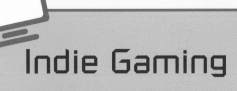

Indie Gaming

Independent or "indie" game developers are individuals or small groups of people who develop video games. Most games take years to develop and are distributed online. One of the most successful indie games was *Minecraft*, created by Swedish developer Markus Persson in 2009.

Riot Games

Riot Games is among the newer game development companies. It was founded in 2006 by Marc Merrill and Brandon Beck. Before starting Riot Games, they had careers in finance and marketing. But both men were also

A *Counter-Strike: Global Offensive* match in progress at the 2017 Dreamhack Masters tournament in Las Vegas

big video game fans. Riot Games is best known for creating *League of Legends*, which was published in 2009. This game allows players to play it free of charge. Players have the option to pay for additional features inside the game.

   League of Legends is a MOBA game. It pits two teams of five players against each other. Players control characters called champions. Champions have special, unique abilities and strengths. In a tournament, two teams use champions to battle each other. The goal is to destroy the other team's main base, called a nexus. *League of Legends* remains one of the most popular MOBA games. Designers created a winning game by continually updating it, often as a result of community feedback. The ever-evolving

DID YOU KNOW?

Riot Games runs a worldwide tournament for *League of Legends.* In 2016, teams from around the world competed in the World Championship held in the United States. The winner of the Summoner's Cup was SK Telecom T1 from South Korea.

Players compete in the 2016 *League of Legends* Continental League finals in Russia.

game stays fresh. The most successful games of today receive frequent updates. Players are challenged to master new skills and polish teamwork.

CHAPTER 5

The Future of E-Sports Game Design

More and more people are enjoying watching E-Sports video games like fans of any other sport. E-Sports are available to view in a variety of ways. Fans can go to actual competitions or watch on devices using live streaming services like Twitch (ages 13 to 18 need a parent or legal guardian's permission) and YouTube. Game designers add elements to ensure the game can be broadcasted and viewed easily by the game's community.

Game developers are opening up the design process to viewers and players. Preview programs encourage fans and players to try games and contribute ideas. Their feedback helps game designers refine games. Designers are experimenting with giving players more room to express themselves through game play. Players can try out strategies and devise their own goals.

Video games are reaching a greater, more diverse audience. Game designers are recognizing this shift. Some believe that more realistic games will attract more players. As more people join the E-Sports community, games are becoming more inclusive of viewers.

Livestream setups are often similar to this one, with a webcam showing the player and a microphone headset for players to communicate with viewers.

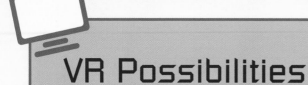

VR Possibilities

Game developer Valve and electronics manufacturer HTC developed a virtual reality headset. In the future, virtual reality may allow viewers to feel as though they are at an E-sports event from the comfort of their own home. Virtual reality headsets might allow viewers to watch a game unfold as a player does. This may mean that designers will create games made for virtual reality.

Virtual and **augmented** reality technologies add an exciting element to game design. Virtual reality allows viewers to have three-dimensional experiences and use their physical bodies to control game movements. Augmented reality adds graphics, sound, and other senses to the existing environment. Graphics can be

DID YOU KNOW?

E-sports have grown in popularity worldwide. Research group Newzoo reported that in 2016, nearly 150 million people around the world were E-sports fans.

made to fit each viewer's perspective.

Most E-Sports games today are played on a console or personal computer. Mobile gaming is very popular with younger players but not as popular for E-Sports.

But mobile games are perfect for connecting with a community of gamers. Many smartphone users already are

Players of virtual reality games wear headsets to be immersed in the virtual world around them.

connected to social media. And with so many smartphone users, it's easy to have a tournament, even if a small percentage of users decides to play. Mobile tournaments are an increasing trend.

Inside *Dota*

For the 2016 *Dota 2* tournament, Valve added its Dota VR Hub. This feature allowed fans to watch games in three virtual reality modes. Fans could feel as though they were flying above the game map, immersed in the game action, or surrounded by other fans in the audience.

The challenge for game developers and designers will be to continue innovating. They will need to use the latest technologies such as mobile gaming and virtual reality to create games that the community will love and want to play. Rising to new challenges is what keeps game design always changing and thriving.

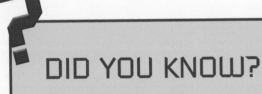

DID YOU KNOW?

Matchmaking systems are very important to a player's enjoyment of a game. Developers try to match players to someone of a similar skill level. This helps ensure a player isn't defeated easily and stops playing the game.

Though not an E-Sports game, *Pokémon GO* is one example of a popular mobile game with augmented reality.

GLOSSARY

arcade

An area or business that has video, pinball, and other games that can be played.

augmented

In game design, to make larger or enhance.

bugs

Errors in a computer program that make it run incorrectly or cause other problems.

consoles

Computer systems that connect to televisions and are made for playing games.

genres

Types or categories of something.

graphics

The images of objects shown on a computer screen.

modes

Different configurations of a game that players can chose to play.

prototype

An early representation of a model that is used for testing.

software

Programs that run on a computer or gaming system.

spectators

People who watch an event.

FOR MORE INFORMATION

Books

Frederick, Shane. *Gamers Unite! The Video Game Revolution.* Mankato, MN: Compass Point Books, 2010.

Jozefowicz, Chris. *Video Game Developer.* Pleasantville, NY: Gareth Stevens Publishing, 2010.

Kaplan, Arie. *The Crazy Careers of Video Game Designers.* Minneapolis: Lerner Publications Company, 2014.

Roesler, Jill. *Online Gaming: 12 Things You Need to Know.* Mankato, MN: 12-Story Library, 2016.

Websites

Develop-Online.net

www.develop-online.net

gamedevmap

www.gamedevmap.com

International Game Developers Association

www.igda.org

INDEX

Cecilia Pinto McCarthy has written several nonfiction books for children. She also teaches environmental science programs at a nature sanctuary. She lives with her family north of Boston, Massachusetts.